The Whistle Primer

Primer

By Peter Pickow.

Cover design by Mike Bell
Cover photography by Peter Wood
Cover diagram by Alison Fenton
Book design by Nina Clayton

Order No. AM 34877
US International Standard Book Number: 0.8256.0268.8
UK International Standard Book Number: 0.7119.0406.5

Exclusive Distributors:
Music Sales Corporation
257 Park Avenue South, New York, NY 10010 USA
Music Sales Limited
8/9 Frith Street, London W1V 5TZ England
Music Sales Pty. Limited
120 Rothschild Street, Rosebery, Sydney, NSW 2018, Australia

Printed in the United States of America by
Vicks Lithograph and Printing Corporation

Amsco Publications
New York/London/Sydney

PREFACE

Whenever I think about the pennywhistle, there comes to mind the saying which many people use to describe the guitar: "It's the easiest instrument to play poorly and the most difficult one to play well." In a way, this old saw can apply to the pennywhistle. I have seen a child pick up the instrument and—with little or no instruction—start playing simple tunes by ear in a matter of minutes. I have also witnessed performances by virtuoso traditional players that would strain the credulousness of a classically trained flautist. Obviously, here is an instrument that can be whatever you want it to be: Playing the whistle can be a simple diversion or a complex art, or anything in between.

I hope that this brief guide will serve to whet your appetite for some of the joys that this peculiar, familiar, and vital little instrument can bring.

CONTENTS

NOTATION

MUSIC

Although a thorough explanation of standard music notation is beyond the scope of this book, rest assured that any symbols peculiar to music written for the pennywhistle will be explained as they occur. In fact, the exercises and tunes are all presented in such a way that you do not really have to know too much about reading music to jump right in: If you go right through from beginning to end, the sharpening of your music-reading skills will be a valuable by-product of learning to play the pennywhistle.

TABLATURE

'Tablature' is a system of notation for a specific instrument that graphically conveys the mechanics of playing the right notes. While standard notation tells you what pitches to play, tablature tells you how to place your fingers to produce them.

The tablature system used in this book is simply a picture of the six holes as they would appear to you if you were looking in a mirror.

If a circle is open (○), then the corresponding hole on the whistle is uncovered. If a circle is filled (●), then the corresponding hole is covered by the correct finger.

Tablature is a concise way to convey pennywhistle fingerings. However, keep in mind that your goal should always be to relate the standard music notation directly to the fingerings. In this way, you will soon be able to read music printed in books other than this one.

GETTING STARTED

Hold the pennywhistle in your left hand so that your index, middle, and ring fingers cover the top three holes. Your fingers should be straight and relaxed (as opposed to arched) so that each hole is effectively sealed by the fleshy pad of the finger (as opposed to the fingertip). In this way, you will find that you need not apply undue pressure to close the holes: Your hand may remain relatively relaxed. This is very important since any tenseness will inhibit the natural agility of your fingers.

Placement of the thumb varies from player to player. Try shifting your thumb up and down the back of the whistle until you find a position that feels natural and well-balanced. If no one position feels best, try placing your thumb directly opposite your middle finger or just slightly higher.

Now you are ready to play. Place the mouthpiece between your lips. Keep your mouth and jaw relaxed in a natural closed positoin. Your teeth should be parted slightly; about the same as for normal speech. Do not let the mouthpiece touch your teeth. Relaxation is the key: If your lips, jaws, fingers, or any other part of your body is tense, your music will also be tense.

Next, whisper the syllable *too* and hold a steady stream of breath. What you will hear is the note G.

If you hear squeaks, or if the pitch wavers, check to make sure that all three fingers are covering the holes completely. Also make sure that you are not 'overblowing'. Experiment with the different amounts of air pressure until you find the correct amount to produce a steady, pure tone. This skill of 'breath control' will soon become second nature.

Here are two more notes, A and B.

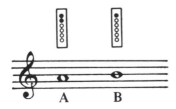

Try stringing all three notes together by going up and down smoothly, slowly, and evenly. Practice this little exercise two ways: First, 'tongue' (whisper *too*) only the first G; then try tonguing each note.

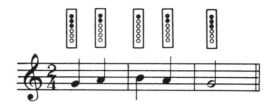

The first version of this exercise is an example of 'slurring'. When you go from one note to the next without tonguing the second note, you have executed a slur. Slurs are indicated by a curved line that connects the two notes or includes a group of three or more notes.

In playing pennywhistle, slurring and tonguing are basic methods of 'phrasing'. Slurring a group of notes tends to link them together while tonguing each note gives a more detached impression. Try playing this example again and listen to the difference it makes whether the notes are tongued or slurred.

Tongue each note

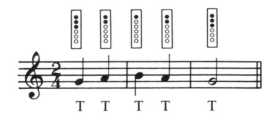

Tongue only the first note

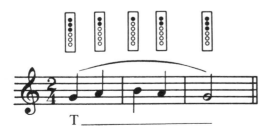

FIRST JIG

In "First Jig" below, be sure to follow the phrase marks and tongue only the first note of each phrase.

(back to the beginning)

THREE MORE NOTES

Now you are ready to bring your right hand into play. Hold the whistle as if to play G. Position your right hand with the index, middle, and ring fingers directly above the bottom three holes. Play G, then bring your right-hand fingers down one at a time, and you will be playing F-sharp*, E, and D.

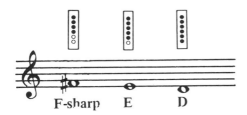

F-sharp E D

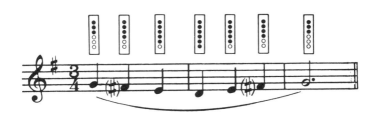

Notice that you have to blow slightly lighter for these lower notes. It is easy to overblow E and D causing them to pop up an octave. However, be careful not to blow too lightly or the pitch will start to waver. Once again, practice the new notes slowly, evenly, and smoothly and the proper breath control will soon become automatic.

Since the pennywhistle is in the key of D Major, the notes in its basic scale are those of the D-Major scale: D E F-sharp G A B C-sharp (D).

FIRST WALTZ

This little waltz uses all of the notes that have been introduced thus far. One thing that might give you some trouble at first is coördinating your fingers in passages where the progression of notes is not scalewise. One of these places is right in the first measure— G to E. Practice going back and forth between G and E until your right-hand index and middle finger move as one. Other places that it would not hurt to practice in this manner are measures seven (B to G to E) and thirteen (E to B). As you play this piece, keep in mind that it is important to keep each finger close to its respective hole. Resist the temptation to let your fingers flap about flamboyantly. Relax and keep each movement small and precise. This will make it easy to play any tune smoothly.

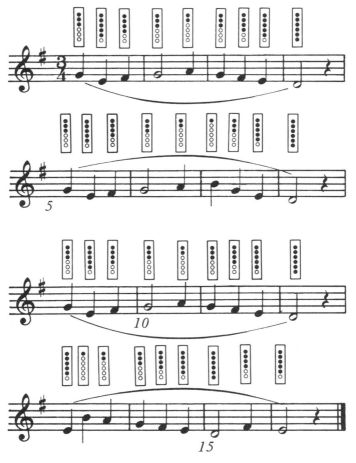

TWO MORE NOTES–
A COMPLETE OCTAVE

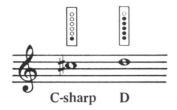

C-sharp   D

Notice that the right-hand ring finger does not make any difference in the pitch or tone of the C-sharp. The only reason for adding it is to help balance the whistle. It is quite often helpful to keep this finger down when playing B and A as well.

With the addition of C-sharp and D, you can now play a one-octave D-Major scale.

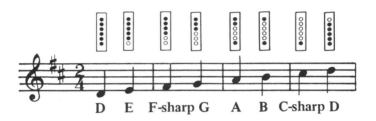

D   E   F-sharp G   A   B   C-sharp D

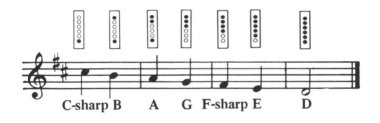

C-sharp B   A   G   F-sharp E   D

FIRST MARCH

This tune introduces a new aspect of articulation: 'double-tonguing'. This may sound pretty fancy but it is simply a very natural way of tonguing repeated notes that would be otherwise difficult to play at tempo.

Play this string of eighth notes but instead of tonguing each one with a whispered too, *alternate between* too *and* koo. *Start slowly and gradually speed up until your tongue is just lightly flicking the steady stream of air.*

T K T K T K T K

Now try this slightly more tuneful exercise. Watch out for the one slur in the sixth and seventh measures.

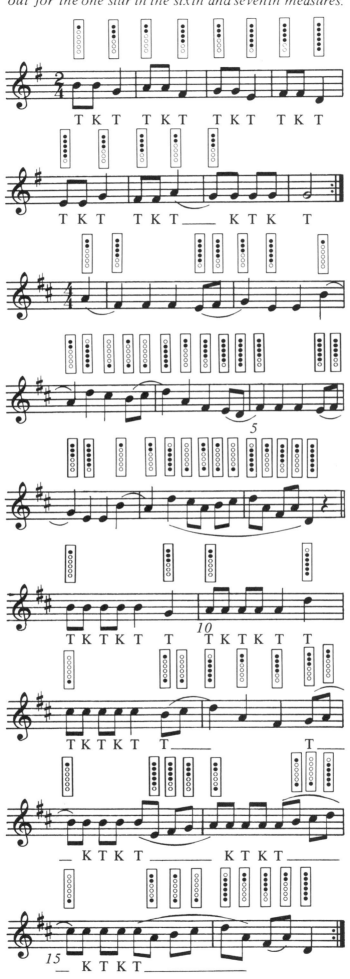

THE REST OF THE NOTES

The high octave of the whistle is fingered the same as the one that you already know. The only difference is that you must blow a little harder to get the notes to pop up. Try this scale in octaves and notice the difference in pressure that is required to produced the high octave.

Do not worry if the high C-sharp and D sound rather shrill: they always do.

To really get down your control of the high octave, play this next exercise as smoothly as possible, taking careful note of the slurs.

FIRST REEL

Before you play this tune, you will have to know about 'grace notes'. These are notes which are printed smaller than regular notes and are not really part of the melody but rather serve to ornament it. Because of this they are just sort of "stuck in" and theoretically take up no time value at all. Actually, they exist by grace of the note which they follow. That is, they are played very quickly just before the note which they ornament. Grace notes and other more intricate ornaments are an important part of traditional Irish whistle-playing. Much of the ornamentation is derived from bagpipe playing and is used to articulate repeated notes without tonguing. (Tonguing is obviously impossible on any type of bagpipe.) In fact, due to the similarity in fingering, the pennywhistle is often used as a considerably quieter preliminary, or alternative, to the highland or uilleann pipes.

Here is a simple example of ornamentation.

Faced with these three F-sharps, you could tongue them individually.

Now try quickly flicking your right-hand index finger up and down instead of tonguing the notes.

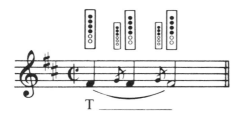

You can also use a grace note from below by flicking your right-hand middle finger down and up.

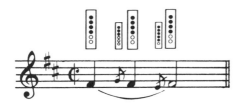

Probably the most common type of grace note is what a bagpiper would call a 'cut'. For this one you leave the lowest finger in place and flick one of the fingers above it up and down.

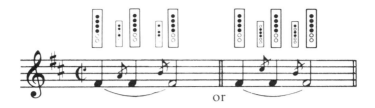

or

Combining the upper and lower grace notes gives you what whistle players refer to as a 'roll'.

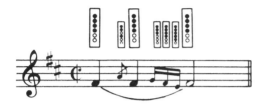

Try this phrase which ends with a combination of grace notes and a roll. Play it all in one breath and notice how much more interesting it sounds than if you were to just tongue the repeated notes.

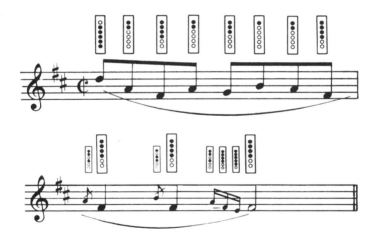

FIRST REEL

Now try "First Reel" with its high-octave work in the first half and ornamentation in the second. Watch for an alternate fingering for C-sharp in the last measure.

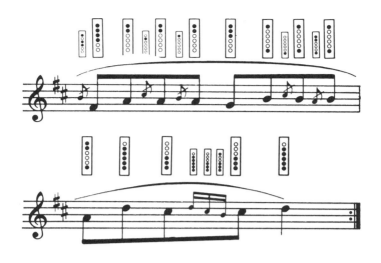

In the tunes that follow, the ornamentation is purposely simple. When first learning a tune, it is often advisable to leave out the grace-note figures until you are able to begin to bring the tune up to speed. When you are ready to insert the ornaments, be sure to follow the fingerings given. More often than not these will sound rather strange if played slowly. Isolate problem spots and work on them until you fully understand how each ornament fits in.

If you are having an inordinate amount of trouble with a specific ornament, try changing it or leaving it out completely. Remember that true ornamentation is a matter of personal style and preference. Try to listen to good pennywhistle players on record or in person. Once you have an idea of what they are doing, you can incorporate any of their tricks or techniques into your own playing. You will find that a good player will change a tune to insert his or her own twists and turns. Some may use virtuostically florid triplet runs; others may use teasing, rippling sequences of double-cut grace notes; still others may play it straight.

Here is one more example of how ornamentation can embellish and personalize a phrase. Say you find this in a tunebook.

These are three ways that you might interpret it. Any one of them—or any combination of any or all of them—might sound good to you.

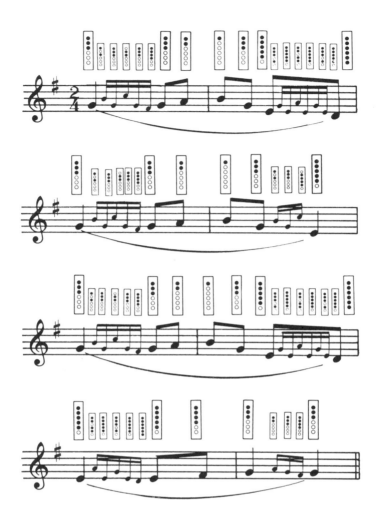

Are there any other ways to play this tune . . .?

THE TUNES

DARGASON

A simple English country-dance tune that may be so much fun to play because it never seems to end. The chord symbols under the music are for guitar, piano, or any other backup instrument. Since most of these tunes can be harmonized in more than one way, you will usually find alternate chord changes in parentheses or written underneath the primary changes.

Time now to embark on some genuine music. If you are fairly confident with the material so far, you should have no trouble with this batch of tunes. Most of them were chosen because I happen to like them, but you can learn something from each one of them. There will be new techniques and tricks introduced in some of them so it is probably a good idea to start at the beginning and read right through. Enjoy.

Traditional

FOOL'S JIG

There are two new phrasing techniques employed in this tune. The first occurs in measure five where you will see a dot above the B. This indicates that the note should be played staccato. Give it slightly less than its full value and thus detach it from the following G.

The other new technique is a 'slide' from the E in measure fourteen to the F-sharp in measure fifteen. Instead of lifting your right-hand middle finger decisively—as you would normally do—let it roll off the hole gradually, causing the pitch to bend up to the F-sharp.

Although many would not consider staccato notes and slides to be techniques of phrasing, they do emphasize certain notes and contribute to the cohesiveness of phrasing of the tune in general.

Bm   D   B7

Em (A7)   D (Bm)   Em
                      E7

A7   D (Bm) (F♯m)

G   (A7)   D   Em
             Bm   E7

A7   D G D   D.C.
Bm
(back to the beginning)

The "Fool's Jig" is an English morris-dance tune used to accompany an intricate solo dance involving the adroit and somewhat hazardous manipulation of a large stick between the dancer's legs. Play it with an up-tempo, almost humorous feel, but not too fast.

OLD MOTHER OXFORD

This is another English morris dance which takes the form of a light-hearted march. Another new phrasing indication appears at the beginning of the B section. From measure seventeen on you will see dashes above or below some of the note-heads. These indicate that you should play these notes with a 'pressure accent'. The feel is similar to staccato in that the main distinction that you should give these notes is detachment from the notes immediately following. However, the pressure accent (also called marcato*) calls for a little extra stress on the affected note.*

Since the last four measures of the A and B sections are identical, I have added a little extra ornamentation the second time around.

RONDEAU

This "Rondeau" is from the first Suite de Symphonies *by Jean-Joseph Mouret, published in 1729. These days it is most certainly better known as "Theme from Masterpiece Theater." It is a fairly straightforward tune; the only tricky part is the high D in measure five.*

Jean - Joseph Mouret
1682 - 1738

D.C. al Fine means to go back to the beginning and play through the tune until you reach the word Fine; *in this case measure sixteen.*

MY LODGING'S ON THE COLD GROUND

This waltz is also known by the name "All Those Endearing Young Charms" after the song of the same title.

There are two fingerings for a new note: C-natural. The first C-natural occurs in measure three. Notice the alternate fingering for the B that follows in measure five which greatly facilitates an otherwise awkward change. To execute the grace-note C-natural in measure six, I have suggested using a 'half-hole' fingering. Simply uncover the top hole halfway, as if you were going to slide up to C-sharp.

Notice that in measure twenty-five, which is a repeat of measure one, the roll takes the place of the eighth-note A.

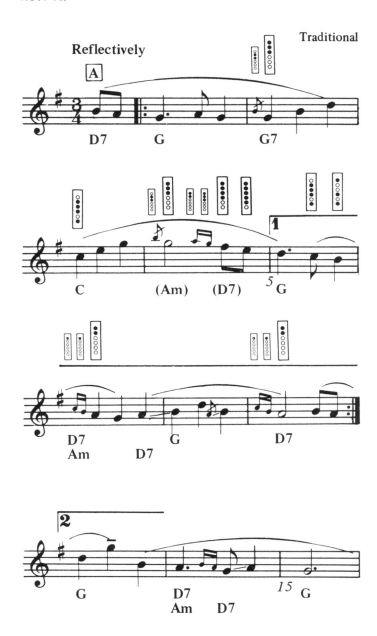

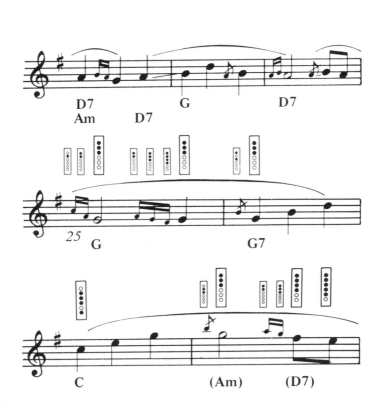

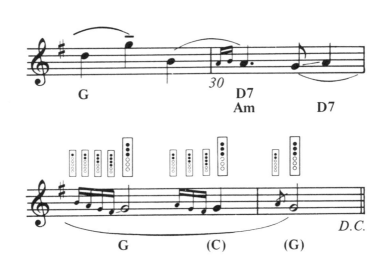

LA RUSSE

Here is a lively little country-dance tune that moves right along. When you practice it slowly, I am sure that all of the ornaments will fit. As you bring it up to speed, you will probably want to be a bit selective about which of them you decide to include. It remains a good tune even without ornaments.

There are a lot of new fingerings in the B section. (Don't let the key change from G to D throw you.) If you follow these alternate fingerings exactly as written, you will be able to see how they make sense: They are all dictated by convenience. If you come up with alternate fingerings that work and make it easier to play the tune, by all means use them.

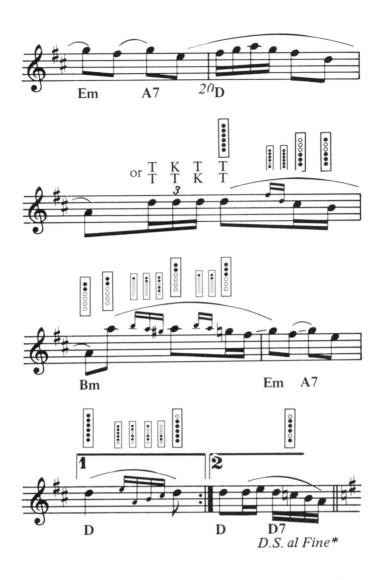

*D.S. al Fine *means to go back to the sign (𝄋) – in this case the first complete measure – and play through the tune until you reach the word* Fine. *Thus once through the complete tune would be A A B B A.*

SHEEBEG SHEEMORE

There is plenty of room for ornamentation in this lovely slow air, but it is best to keep it fairly simple: A few well-placed slides and grace notes will keep it moving but will not detract from the simple, elegant beauty.

Notice that in the grace-note figure in measure ten that the fingering given for the high C-sharp actually produces the note B. There is a similar situation in the last measure in which the fingerings for grace-note G actually produce the tone F-sharp; although the effect is somewhat rougher and more pleasing than a simple alternation between D and F-sharp.

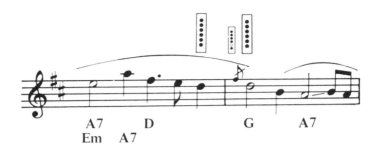

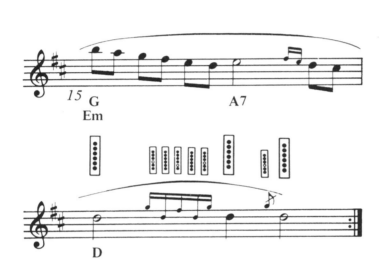

NEWCASTLE

This seemingly simple tune actually allows for quite a range of expression. Try different approaches to the phrasing but always keep it lyrical. There is a symbol in measures seven and twenty-three with which you may not be familiar: The small tr above the staff stands for 'trill'. This means that you should alternate the written note with the note just above, starting with the higher note. Here is the measure as written and as it would be played.

Gently, but not too slow   Traditional

EIGHTH OF JANUARY

"Eighth of January" is a good old American reel known by many as the tune to the song "The Battle of New Orleans." The B section is written out twice with the repeat being an octave higher.

The special fingerings in measures four and eleven are suggestions for "cheating": necessary in this fast a tune.

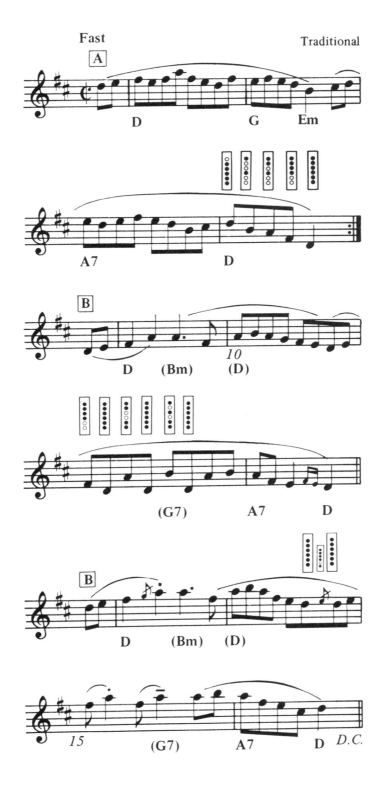

FASTEN THE LEG IN HER

This title is one of my all-time favorites in the seemingly limitless catalogue of fanciful Irish tune names. The tune itself is a grand one and moves right along at a good clip.

In measure twenty-one you will find another example of how rolls may be used to alter the actual notes (contrasted with measure seventeen) and yet maintain, even enhance, the melodic integrity. Speaking of ornaments, you will probably notice that the fingerings given for the C-natural grace notes in measures one, three, five, and nineteen are really C-sharp fingerings. When the tune is played up to tempo, these go by so fast that they do not clash but merely provide the articulation for the repeated note.

WHITE COCKADE

"White Cockade" is a neat Scottish march that should be played with a lilt, but not too fast.

Traditional

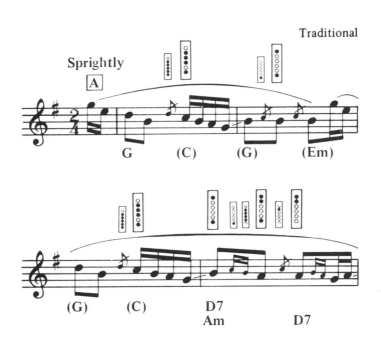

G   (C)   (G)   Em

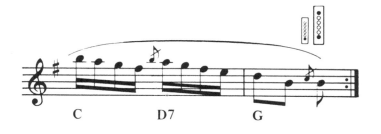

C   D7   G

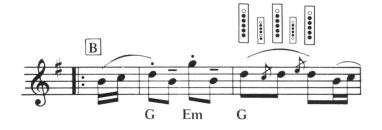

G   Em   G

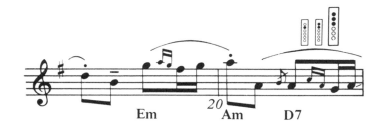

Em   Am   D7

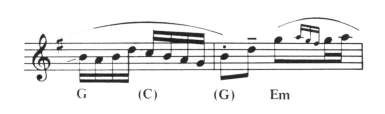

G   (C)   (G)   Em

C   D7   G

BEAN SETTING

A tune for a traditional English morris dance with a funny time-change. It may seem awkward at first but I hope that this explanation will help you to get the right feel: If you look at the first measure of the B section, you will see a half note and a dotted quarter-note separated by an equal sign. This marking tells you that the dotted quarter-note pulse of the B section should be equivalent to the half-note pulse of the A section (except slightly faster).

"Bean Setting" introduces yet another fingering for C-natural. This one is not as true as the 'forked' fingering but is obviously useful in the B-to-C or C-to-B change, as in measures two and four. Whenever it is logical, continue to use the usual fingering, as is indicated in the B section.

Traditional

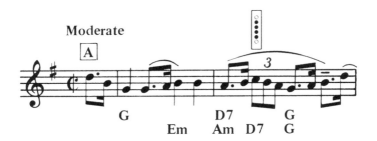

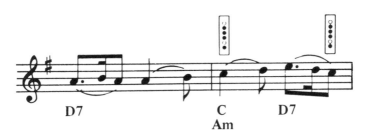

THE RISING OF THE MOON

Here is one of the famous songs of Irish resistance. I have given you the first verse and the chorus as they would be sung. Additional verses follow.

Traditional

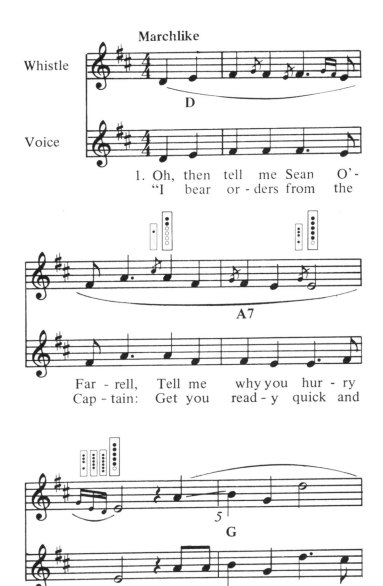

G   Chorus   Bm

glow.   By   the   ris - ing   of   the
moon."

A7

moon, By   the   ris - ing   of   the

20   G

moon.   For the   pikes must be   to -

D

geth - er,   By   the

A7   D

ris - ing   of   the   moon.

2. *Oh then tell me Sean O'Farrell*
   Where the gathering is to be.
   "In the old spot by the river
   Right well known to you and me.
   One more word for signal token
   Whistle up the marching tune
   With your pike upon your shoulder
   By the rising of the moon."

Chorus:
   By the rising of the moon
   By the rising of the moon.
   With your pike upon your shoulder
   By the rising of the moon.

3. *Out of many a mud-wall cabin*
   Eyes were watching through the night.
   Many a manly heart was throbbing
   For the coming morning light.
   Murmurs ran along the valley
   Like the banshees lovely croon
   And a thousand pikes were flashing
   By the rising of the moon.

Chorus:
   By the rising of the moon
   By the rising of the moon.
   And a thousand pikes were flashing
   By the rising of the moon.

4. *There beside the singing river*
   That dark mass of men were seen.
   Far above their shining weapons hung
   Their own beloved green.
   Death to every foe and traitor
   Forward strike the marching tune
   And hurrah me boys for freedom:
   Tis the rising of the moon.

Chorus:
   Tis the rising of the moon
   Tis the rising of the moon.
   And hurrah me boys for freedom:
   Tis the rising of the moon.

THE NUTTING GIRL

A Major is an unusual key for the D pennywhistle because it necessitates the use of the note G-sharp. When you must play a note that is not part of the D-Major scale, you can always find it by half-holing. However, it is often advisable to use the indicated alternate fingerings for G-sharp in up-tempo tunes such as "The Nutting Girl." These fingerings may sound a bit out of tune but they give a more definite impression than half-hole fingerings which are decidedly difficult to hit square-on.

Traditional

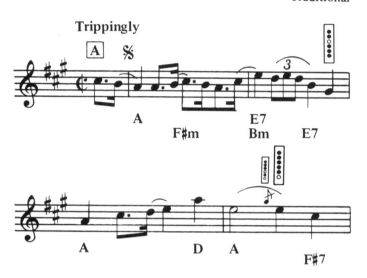

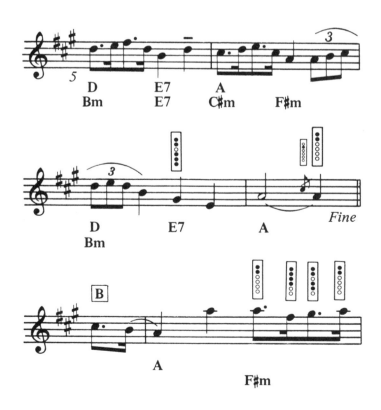

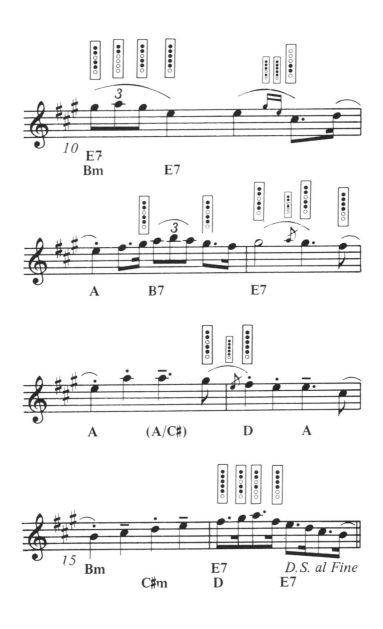

STONE GRINDS ALL

This march comes from a somewhat unusual source: It is taken from a tunebook put together by young Giles Gibbs, Jr. in 1777. I suppose that you could argue that this is an American tune, although it does sound quite British.

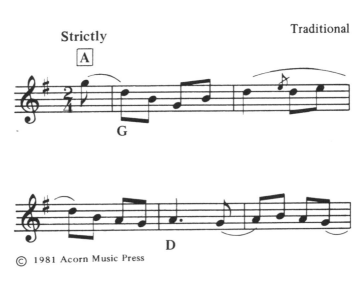

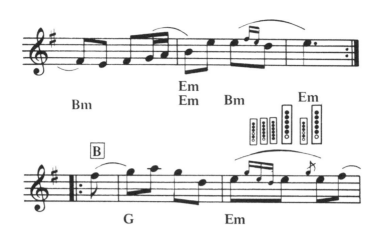

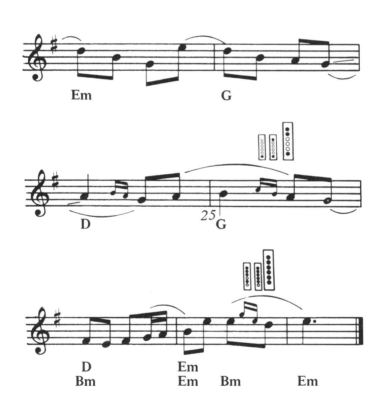

SHEPHERDS' HEY

This unassuming morris-dance tune gives you a good opportunity to practice your C-naturals. In the A section, keeping the right-hand index and ring fingers down—as shown in the tablature—will help smooth out the awkwardness of the various changes involving C-natural.

By the by, a 'hey' in this case is not a boisterous interjection but rather a complex three-man figure-eight that forms the main part of this particular dance.

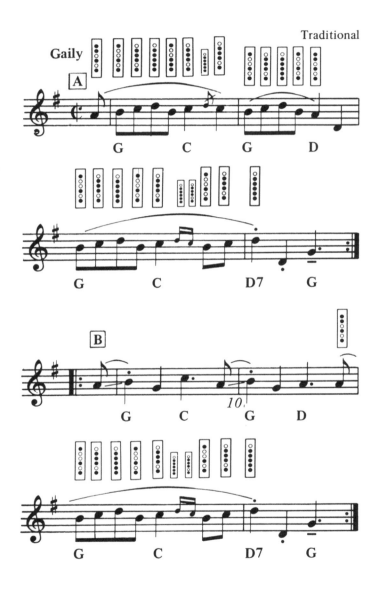

KEVIN BARRY

A wonderfully melodramatic slow air. The song tells a sad, dignified story and the tune should be played in a similar manner.

There is a new technique here that proves very effective in slow tunes. It is a type of 'vibrato' that is obtained by rapidly covering and uncovering one of the open holes that is two or three holes below the lowest hole covered for the given note. This produces a variation in timbre but not in pitch. This vibrato works better for some notes than others and is generally called for only on long, held notes near the end of phrases. It is indicated in the music by the abbreviation 'vib.'. The extra fingering diagram tells you which finger performs the vibrato.

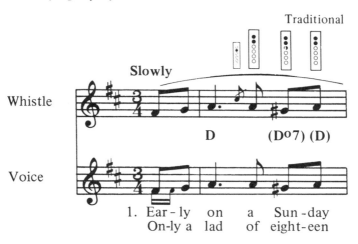

1. Ear-ly   on   a   Sun-day
   On-ly a lad   of   eight-een

morn-ing, high up   on   a   gal-lows
sum-mers, Yet there's   no   one can de-

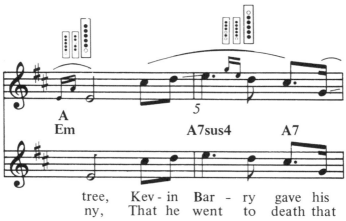

tree,   Kev-in   Bar - ry   gave his
ny,   That he went   to   death that

young   life,   For the cause   of   lib – er –
morn - ing,   Nob-ly

ty.   held   his   head   up   high:

Chorus: (same music as the verse)

"Shoot me like an Irish soldier;
Do not hang me like a dog
For I fought for Ireland's
  freedom
On that dark September morn.
All around that little bakery
Where we fought them hand
  to hand. . .
Shoot me like an Irish soldier
For I fought to free Ireland."

2. Just before he faced the hangman
   In his lonely prison cell
   British soldiers tortured Barry
   Just because he would not tell
   All the names of his companions;
   Other things they wished to know:
   "Turn informer and we'll free
     you."
   Proudly Barry answered, "No!"

Chorus:

3. Calmly standing to attention
   While he bade his last farewell
   To his broken-hearted mother
   Whose grief no one can tell.
   For the cause he proudly
     cherished
   This sad parting had to be.
   Then to death walked softly
     smiling
   That old Ireland might be free.

Chorus:

4. Another martyr for old Ireland
   Another murder for the crown!
   Brutal laws to crush the Irish
   Cannot keep their spirit down.
   Lads like Barry are no cowards
   From the foe they will not fly.
   Lads like Barry will free Ireland
   For her sake they'll live and die.

Chorus:

CRIPPLE CREEK

An ever-popular tune especially with old-time banjo players.

There are some sexy, syncopated slides off of a half-holed F-natural in the B section: Play them with a leer.

Once again, I have given you the B section twice through with the repeat an octave higher.

Traditional

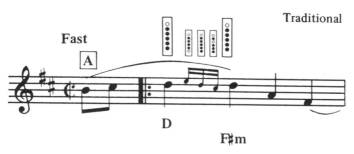

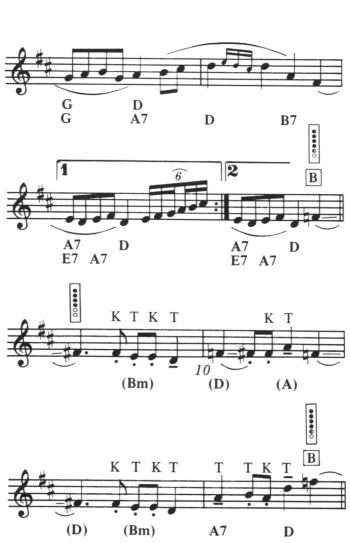

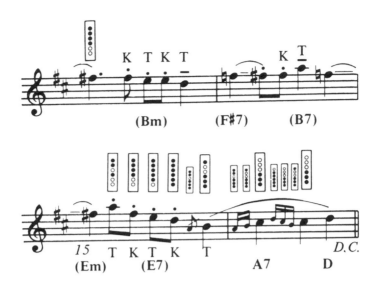

BLARNEY PILGRIM

Here is a well known Irish jig with pretty authentic ornamentation. There are considerably fewer fingering reminders in this one as you have seen it all before by now.

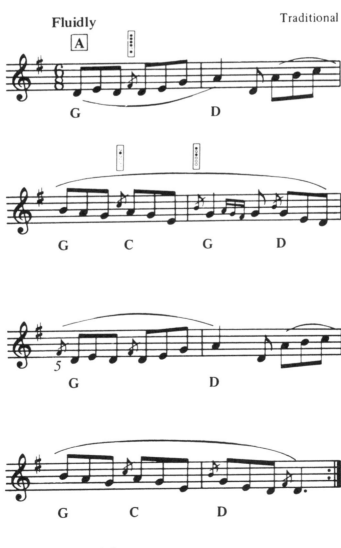

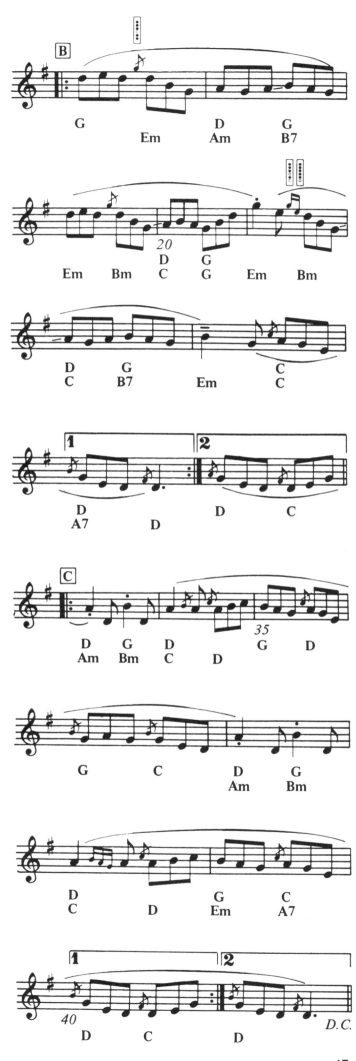

MONEY MUSK

This is a relatively easy contra-dance tune which is a favorite at dances in New England. Although I say it is easy, there is still considerable room for variation in ornamentation, phrasing, and harmony.

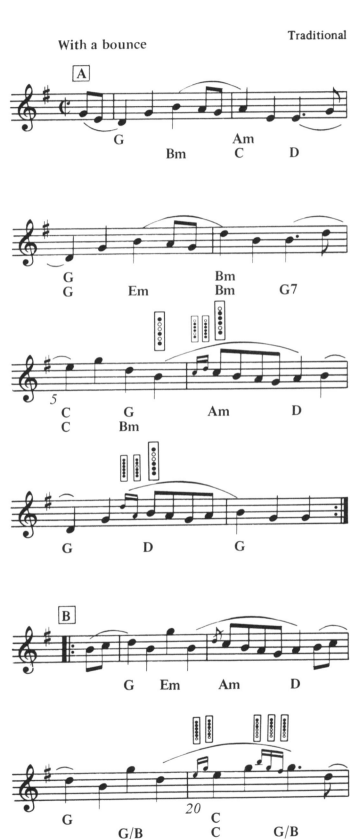

C   G   Am   D
Bm

G   D   G

THE WIND THAT SHAKES THE BARLEY

Another name for this tune is "The Little Pack o' Tailors" which comes from the following set of words.* These words are sung in Ireland as a kind of 'mouth music' when people want to dance and there are no instrumentalists available (or maybe when the musicians want to dance one). The point is obviously to provide rhythmic vitality and good humor rather than an overabundance of rational meaning.

*This song is based on a fragment collected in 1952 from Elizabeth Cronin of County Cork, Ireland by Jean Ritchie and George Pickow. New and additional words by Jean Ritchie, copyright and published by Geordie Music Publishing, ASCAP. All Rights Reserved. Used by Permission.

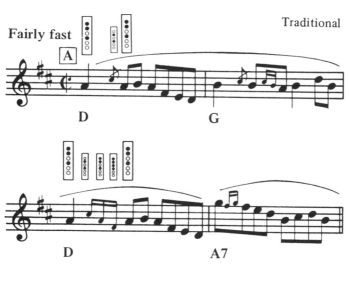

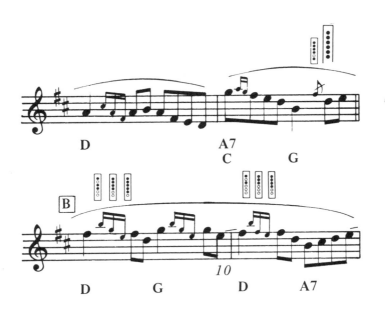

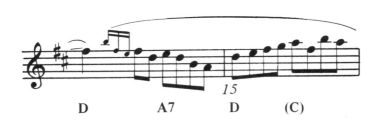

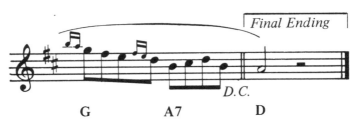

Tow-row we rattled 'em
And tow-row we chased 'em.
Tow-row we rattled 'em
The little pack o' tailors.

I went down to Dublin
I met a little tailor.
Put him in my pocket
In fear the dog 'ud eat him.

Dogs began to bark at him
And I began to beat 'em.
I threw him in the water
In fear the dogs 'ud eat him.

Tow-row we rattled 'em
And tow-row we chased 'em.
Tow-row we rattled 'em
The little pack o' tailors.

Divil caught the tailor;
He caught 'im 'round the middle.
Wouldn't turn him loose until
He played upon the fiddle.

Tailor wouldn't listen and
The tailor wouldn't parley
So the divil stole the fiddle
And he played the "Stack o' Barley"!

ANOTHER JIG WILL DO

Another Jig Will Do and *Drops of Brandy*

These two tunes are 'slip jigs'. A slip jig is written in $\frac{9}{8}$ time. While regular (or 'double') jigs have two pulses of three eighth-notes per bar, a slip jig has three. It is a tricky rhythm to feel at first but tunes such as these have such a flowing, never-ending quality that it soon becomes quite natural. Start out slowly and make sure that you are feeling the tunes in three: one-two-three, two-two-three, three-two-three, *etc.*

Traditional

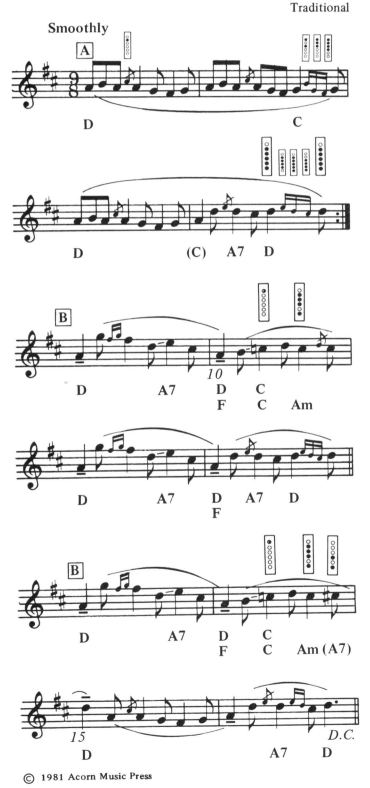

DROPS OF BRANDY

Traditional

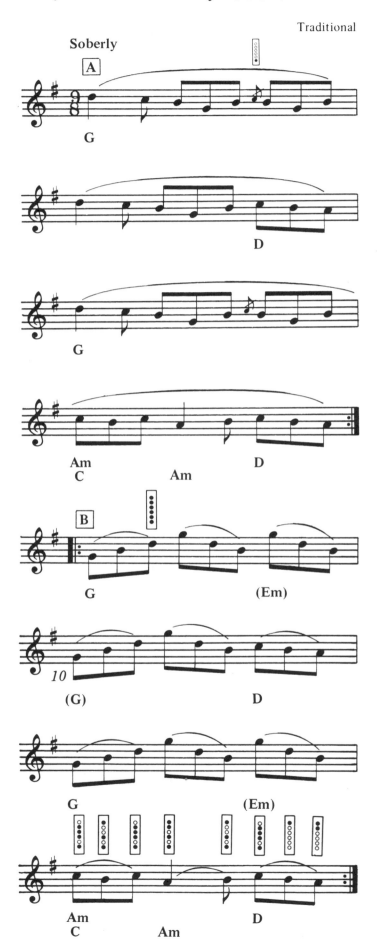